The Story of The Resurrection

As told by

Pastor Chuck Smith

WITH ILLUSTRATIONS BY JOHN SHAFFER

The Word For Today, P.O. Box 8000, Costa Mesa, CA 92628 • Web Site: www.twft.com • E-mail: info@twft.com

The Story of The Resurrection
By Chuck Smith
With illustrations by John Shaffer
Editing by Shannon Woodward and Cheryl Brodersen

Published by The Word For Today
P.O. Box 8000, Costa Mesa, CA 92628
Web site: http://www.twft.com
(800) 272-WORD (9673)

ISBN: 978-1-59751-106-3

Scriptural quotations are based on the King James Version of the Bible. Translational emendations, amplifications and paraphrases are by the author.

Printed in the United States of America.

A special thanks to the following for their voice talent in the audio recording of this book:

- Cheryl Brodersen
- John Henry Corcoran
- Lenya Heitzig
- Skip Heitzig
- Jack Hibbs
- Jeff Johnson
- Damian Kyle
- Greg Laurie
- Mike MacIntosh
- Don McClure
- Jean McClure
- Lloyd Pulley
- Raul Ries
- David Rosales
- Marie Rosales
- Wayne Taylor

THIS IS A STORY about Jesus. Parts of this story are sad, but it also shows us just how much God loves us. And you can't help but be happy when you learn that.

From the beginning of time, God had a plan for how we could be His children. But there was a big, big problem. That problem was our sin nature. God is perfect and holy, and anyone who sins cannot be in His presence.

Before Jesus came to earth, the people paid for their sin with the death of an animal. They would bring a lamb to the priest who would kill it. By doing this, the sins of the people would be covered.

What makes it even sadder is that the people had to do this every year. Year after year, lamb after lamb.... Isn't it sad that a lamb had to die for people's sins?

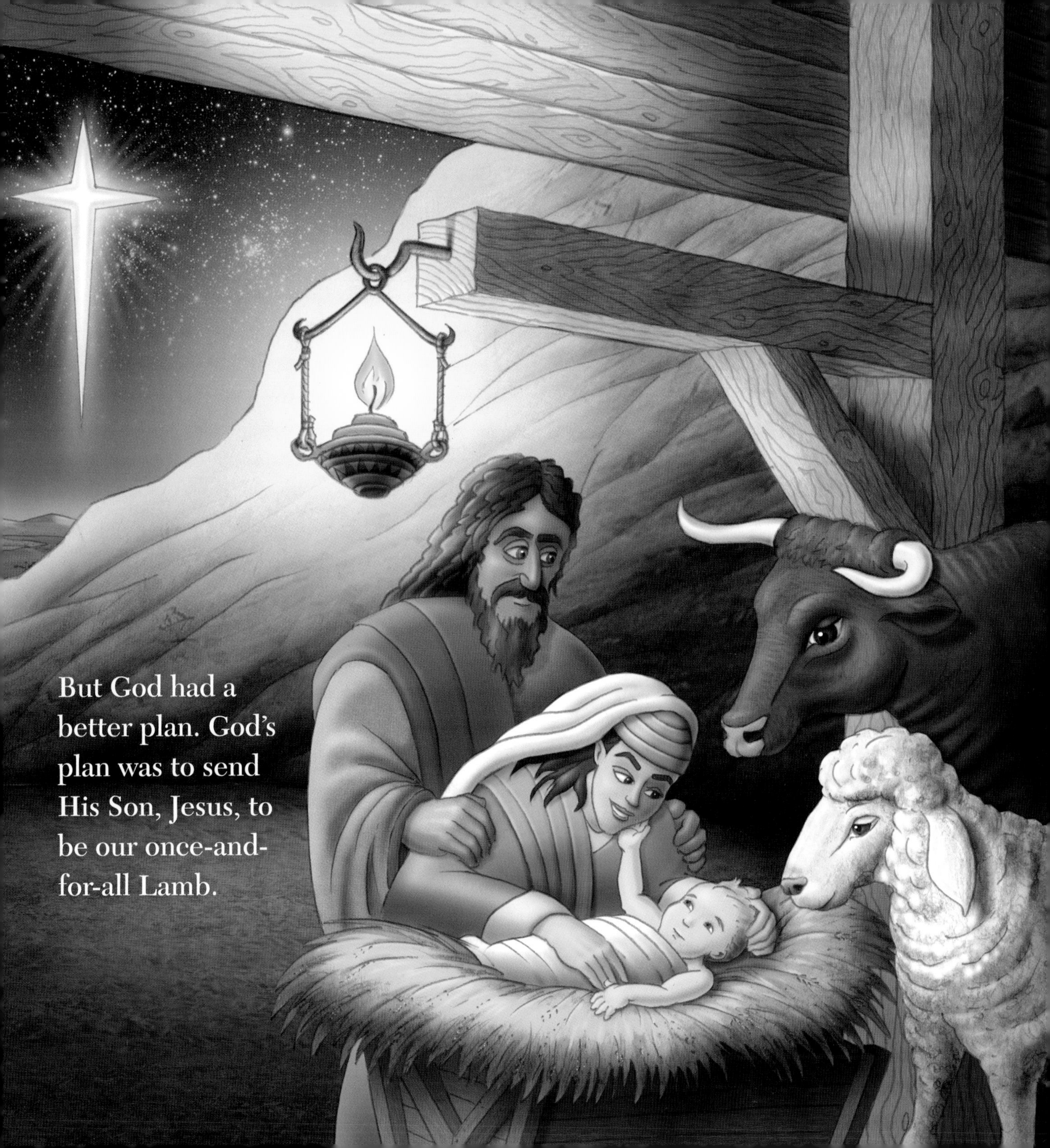

But God had a better plan. God's plan was to send His Son, Jesus, to be our once-and-for-all Lamb.

Jesus knew that He had to come to earth to die for us. He tried to tell His disciples so they'd be ready for that day. He told them He'd be crucified, and then buried, but He would rise again on the third day.

But the disciples didn't understand. Peter even tried to argue with Jesus. "Don't say that! That's not right." Jesus said, "Peter, you don't understand God's plan." He also told Peter, "This very night, before the rooster crows, you will deny Me three times."

Not long after, the soldiers came and arrested Jesus. They took Him away, and treated Him very harshly.

Peter stood outside the court listening to what was happening to Jesus. A little girl was there too, and she asked Peter, “Aren’t you one of His disciples?” Peter was scared, so he said, “No, I’m not.”

Soon
another girl
walked up to
Peter, saying,
"Hey, I saw you
with Jesus. You are
one of His disciples."
Again, Peter denied this.
"No, you're wrong.
I don't even know Him."

Then a group of people who were nearby walked over to Peter. "Surely you are one of His disciples." Peter got very angry. "I am not! I am not!" he cried out.

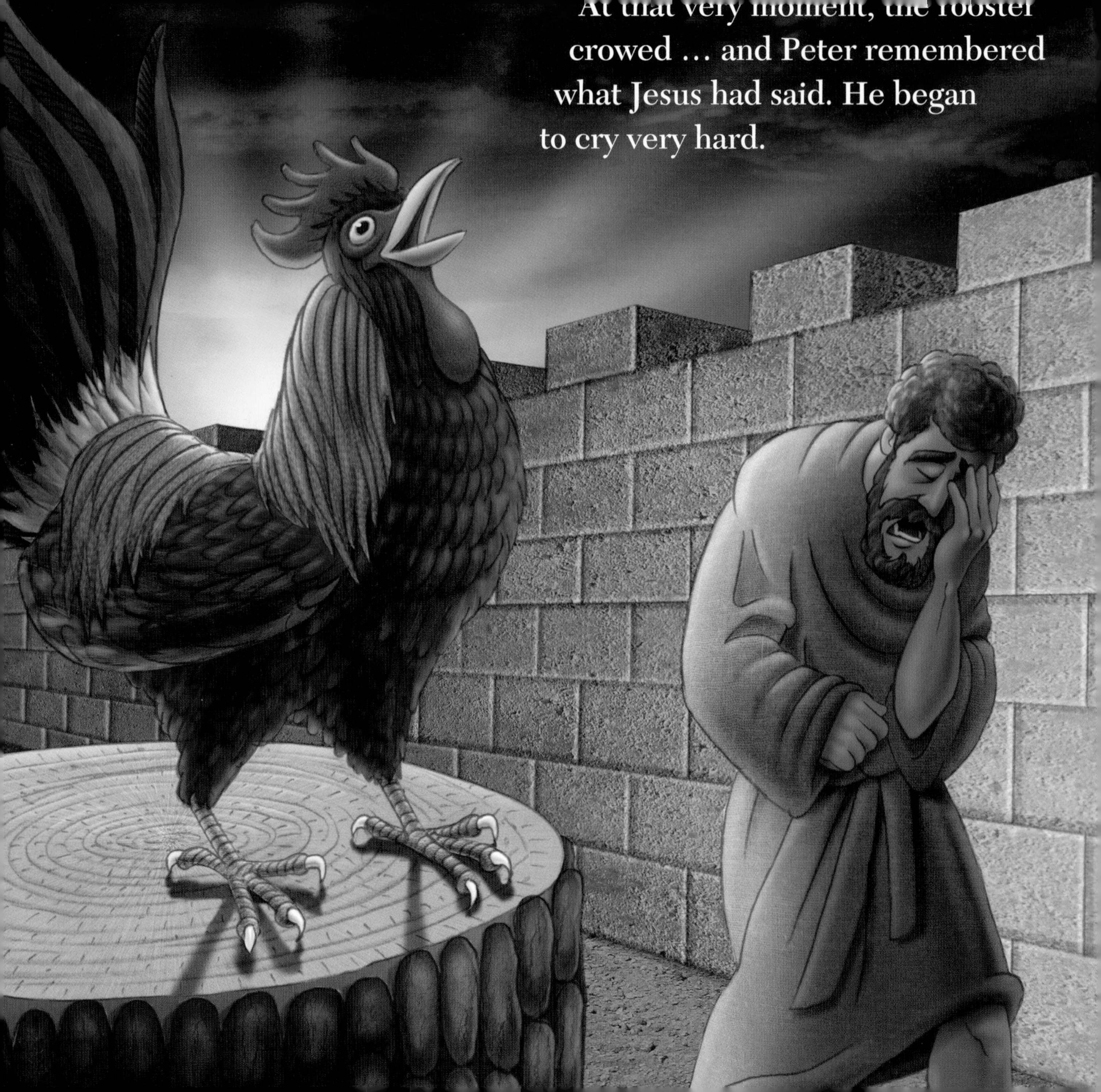

At that very moment, the rooster crowed … and Peter remembered what Jesus had said. He began to cry very hard.

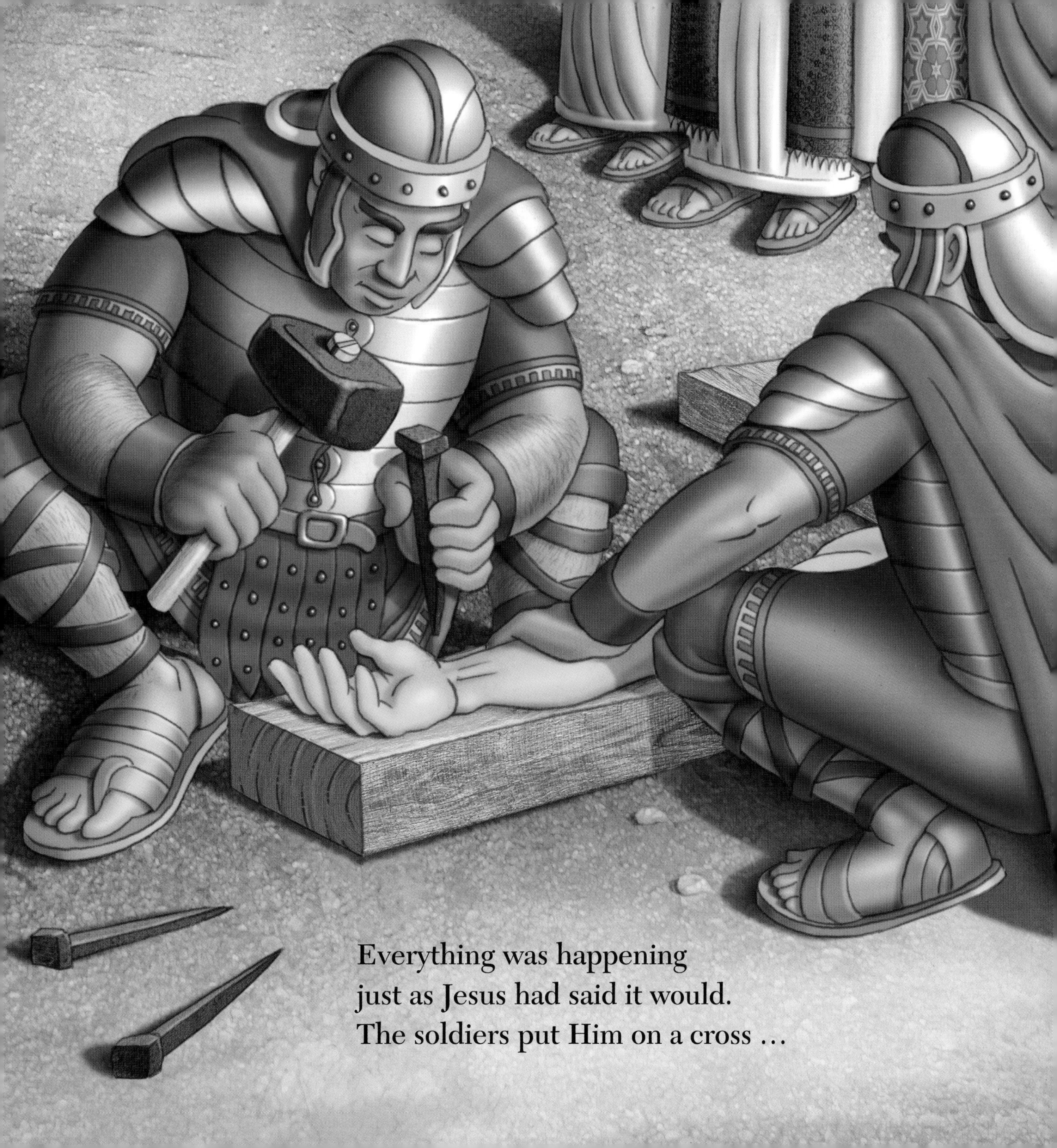

Everything was happening
just as Jesus had said it would.
The soldiers put Him on a cross …

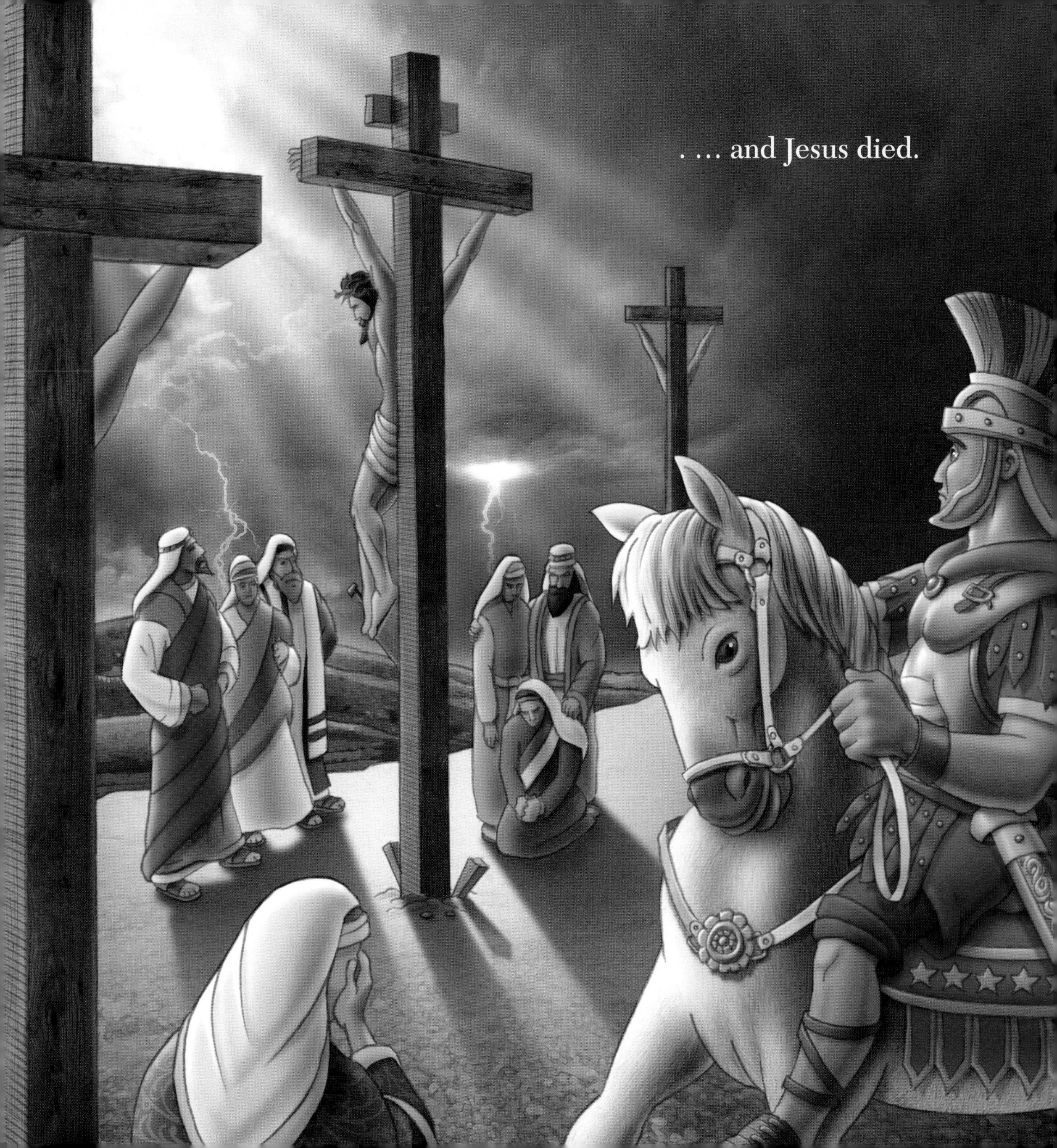

. … and Jesus died.

They laid His body
in a tomb, and rolled a
giant stone in front to keep
people out. Jesus' friends and
disciples wept. "He's dead.
What are we going to do?"
They didn't know how
they could go on
without Jesus.

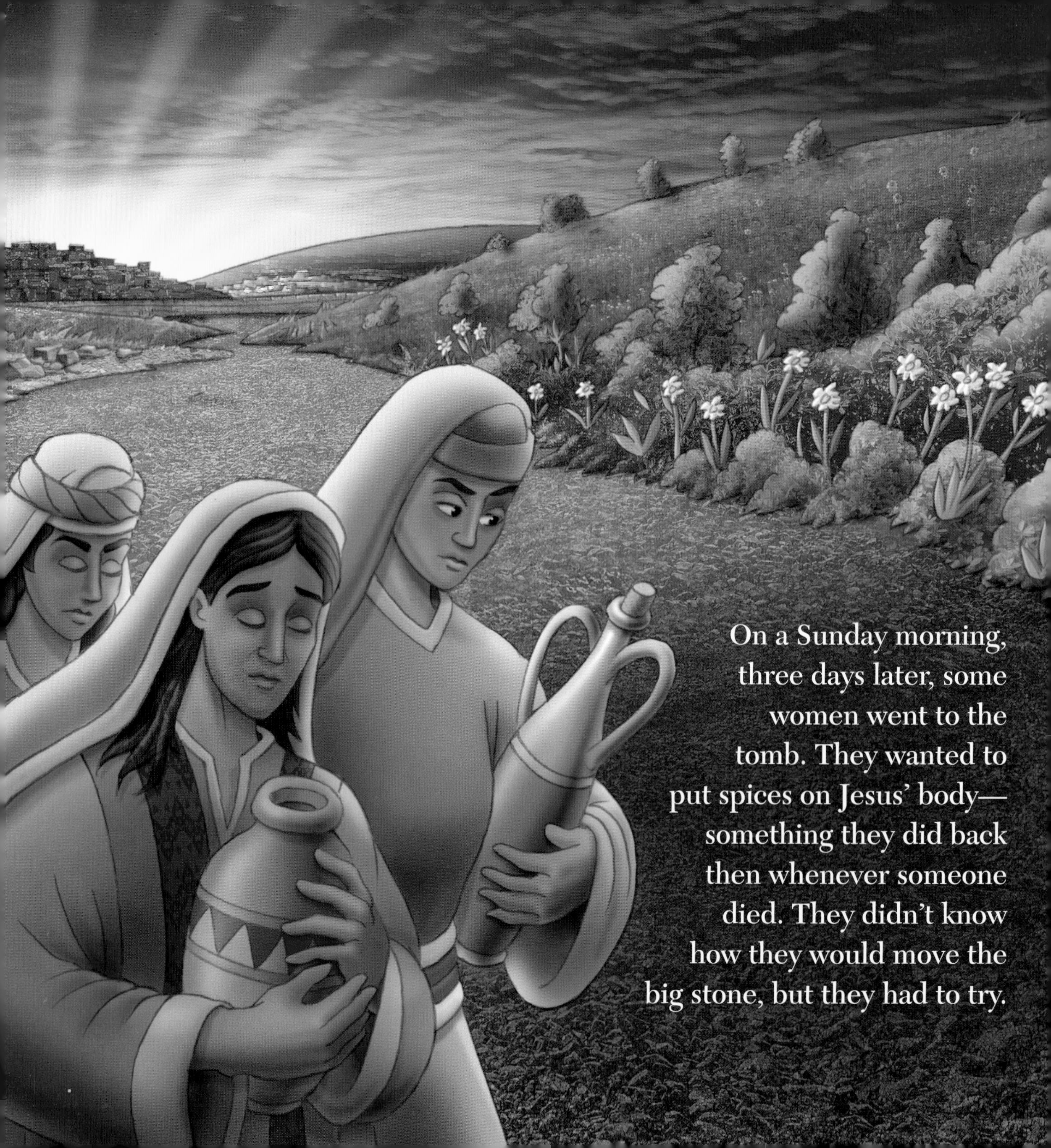

On a Sunday morning, three days later, some women went to the tomb. They wanted to put spices on Jesus' body—something they did back then whenever someone died. They didn't know how they would move the big stone, but they had to try.

Guess what they saw when they reached the tomb? The great, big stone had been rolled away!

The women peeked inside the tomb and saw two angels. "Why are you seeking the living among the dead?" one of the angels asked. "He is not here. He is risen from the dead, just like He said."

The angels told the women to run and tell the disciples the good news. Oh, how those women ran! Peter and John decided to go see for themselves. The Bible tells us that John ran faster than Peter! Guess who got to the tomb first?

John and Peter looked inside and saw that the tomb was empty and that the linens that had been wrapped around the body of Jesus were all still there … but the napkin that had been over His head was neatly folded.

It was true! Jesus had risen from the dead! There was great rejoicing among the disciples that day. But not everyone believed.

Two of the disciples who doubted were walking to a place called Emmaus, when Jesus suddenly joined them. “Why do you look so sad?” He asked. They didn’t realize it was Jesus.

"You must be new around here," they said. "Otherwise you would know what happened." They told Jesus about the crucifixion, and the women who said He had risen. But they didn't believe.

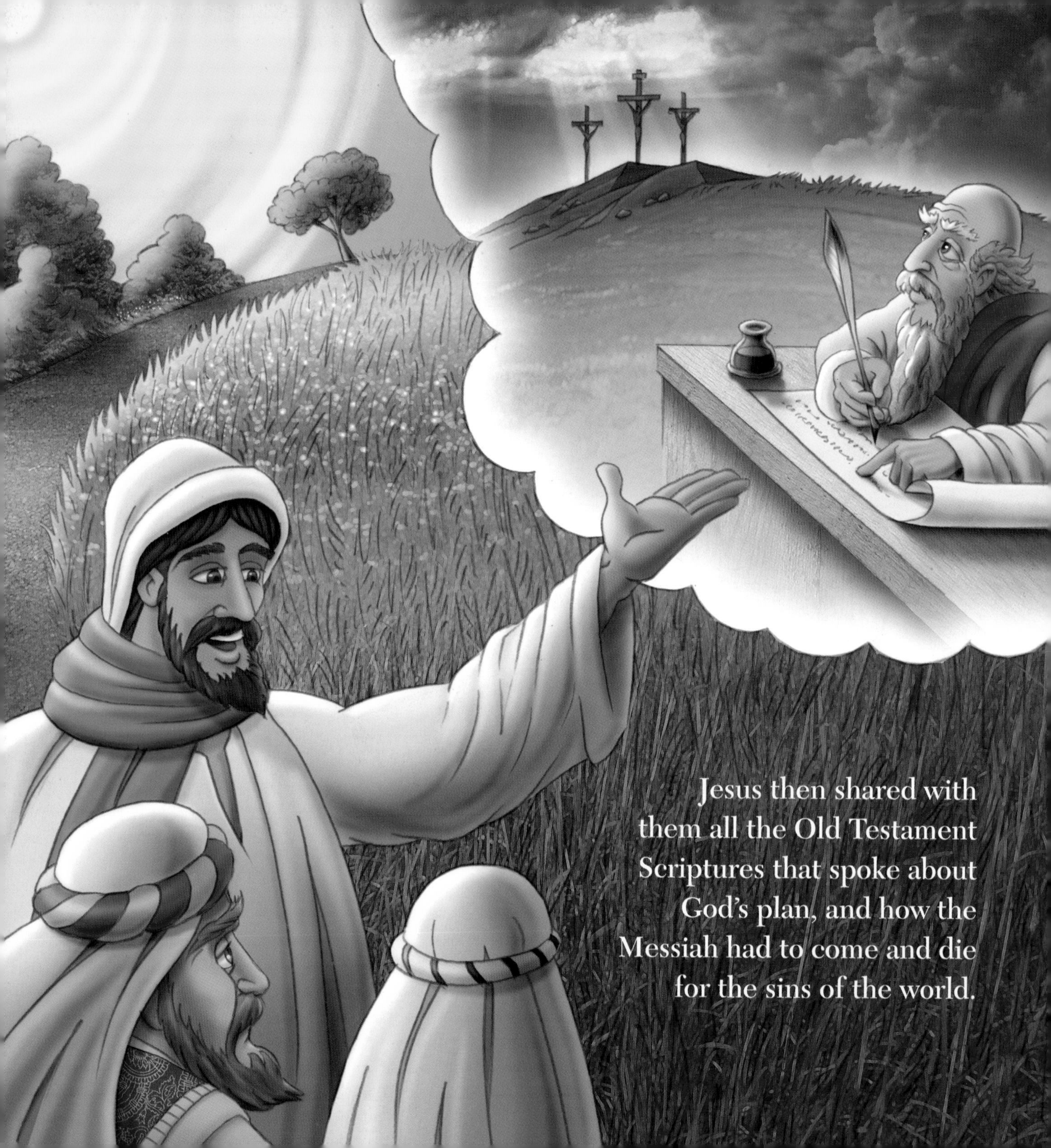

Jesus then shared with them all the Old Testament Scriptures that spoke about God's plan, and how the Messiah had to come and die for the sins of the world.

When they reached Emmaus, the disciples said, "It's getting late. Come and eat with us." When Jesus took the bread and broke it, the disciples saw the marks on His hands where He had been nailed to the cross. They recognized Him! Then Jesus disappeared.

Over the next forty days, lots of people saw Jesus. Even doubting Thomas, a disciple of Jesus, believed after he touched the scars on Jesus' hands and side. He said, "Oh, my Lord and my God!"

One day when Peter and his friends were fishing in a boat, they saw Jesus cooking breakfast on the shore. Peter jumped in the water and swam to the shore.

As Peter sat talking with Jesus, three times Jesus asked, "Peter, do you love Me?" Three times Peter answered, "You know I do, Lord." And three times Jesus told him, "Feed My sheep."

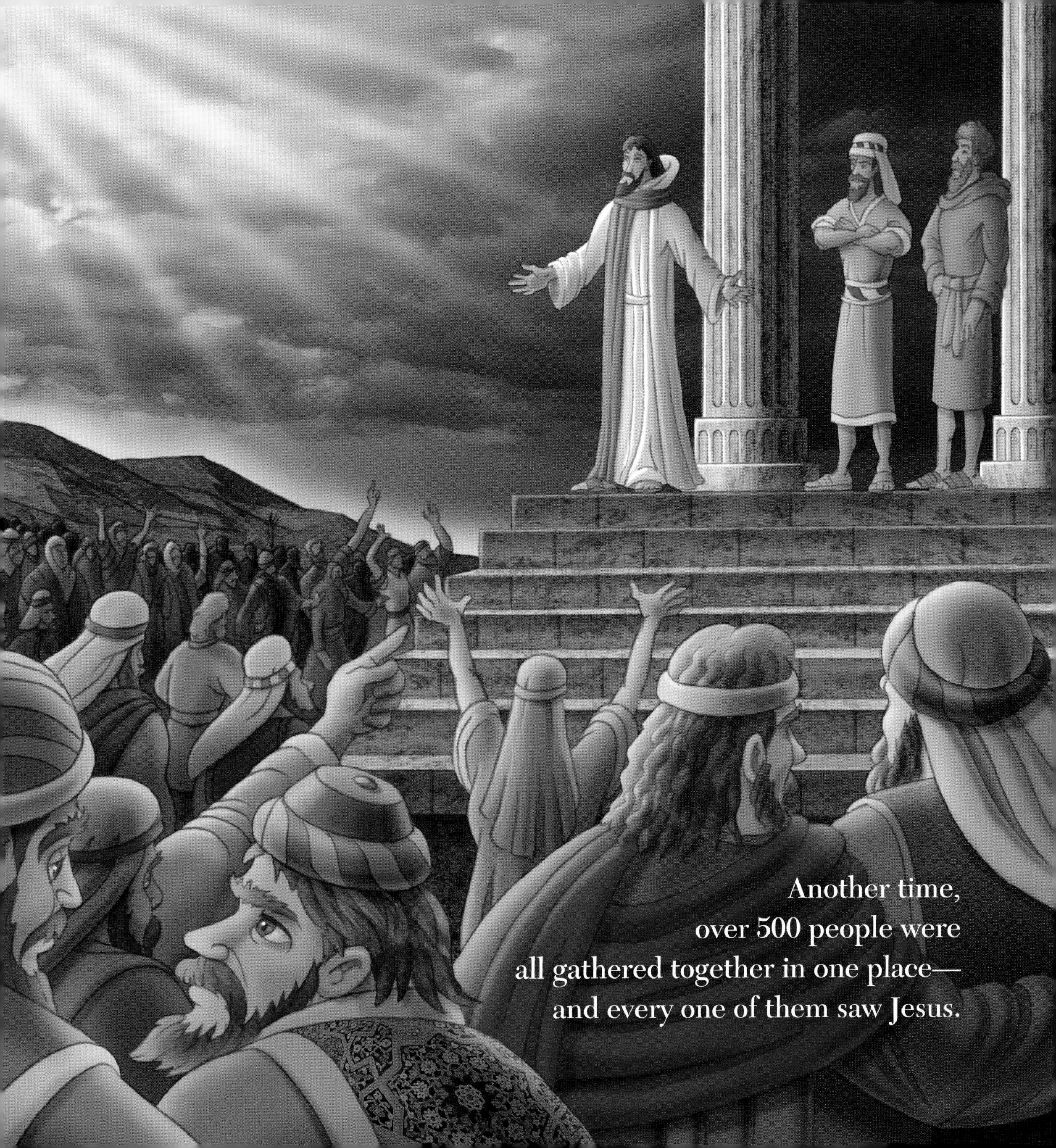

Another time,
over 500 people were
all gathered together in one place—
and every one of them saw Jesus.

One afternoon
as Jesus walked with His
disciples to the Mount of Olives,
which is next to Jerusalem,
He lifted up His hands and
blessed them. Then right
before their eyes, He went up
to heaven in a cloud.

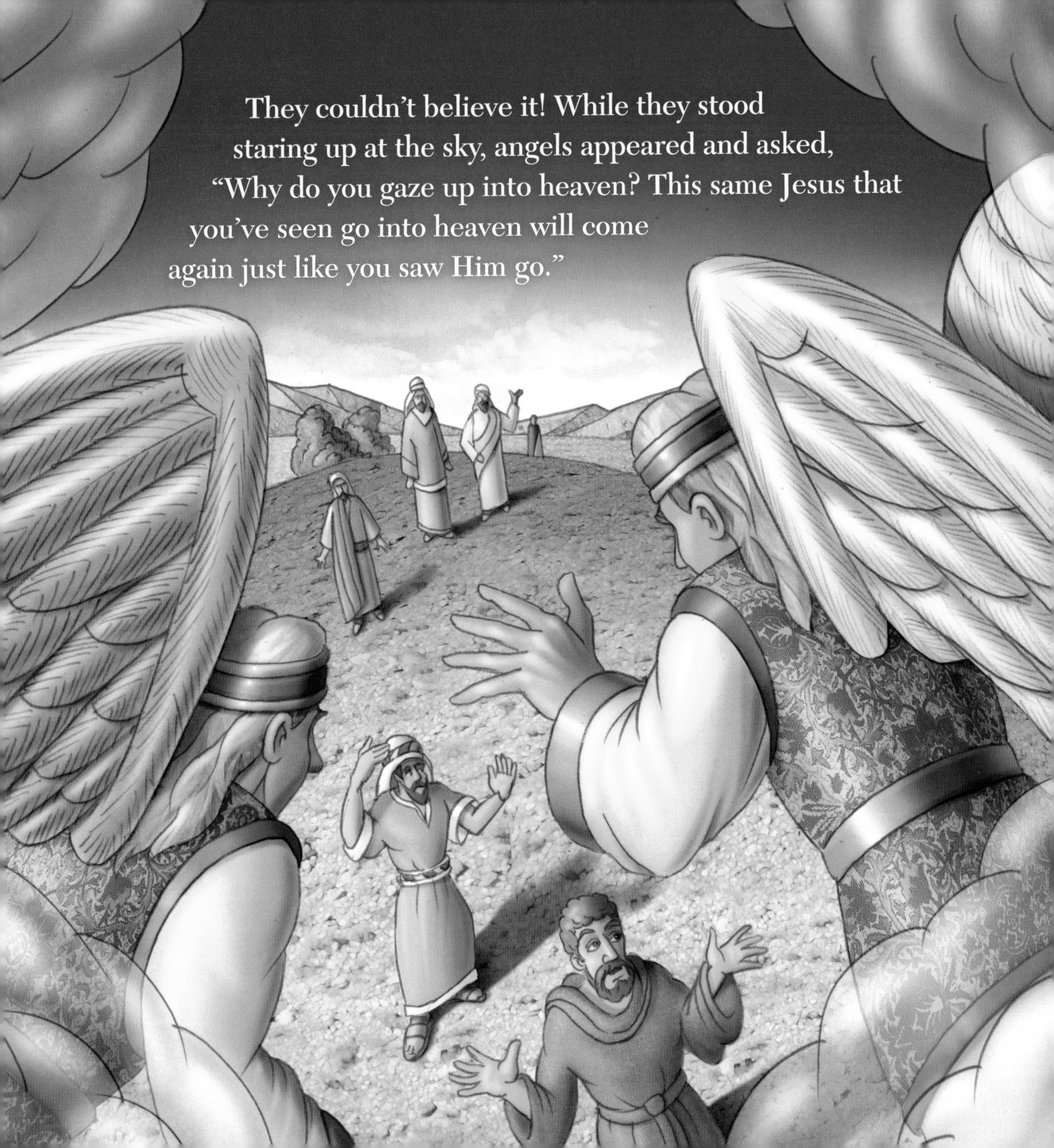

They couldn't believe it! While they stood staring up at the sky, angels appeared and asked, "Why do you gaze up into heaven? This same Jesus that you've seen go into heaven will come again just like you saw Him go."

That's the story of the resurrection and it's the most important story in the Bible. Jesus is alive today, and one day very, very soon, He's going to come back for us. Jesus promised it, and whatever He says, He does. Amen!

The End